My Caribbean Run

_By_
Dale "Catman" Ballard

This is a true story, unfolding over the course of November and December 1977. I was just 19 years old, a year and a half out of high school, and working a typical job in northern Indiana. Life was ordinary, uneventful—until everything changed with a phone call.

My mom and her boyfriend, Roy-Boy, had taken off for Ft. Lauderdale, Florida, a few months earlier. They had found work on a boat with some friends, and although we stayed in touch, I never really knew the full extent of what was happening down there. I only got bits and pieces, fragments of their new life. Then came the call that would set everything in motion.

It was Thursday, November 10, when my mom called me. Her voice was full of excitement as she asked if I'd be interested in coming down to Florida to "work on the boat." At first, I was puzzled. Why me? I was only 19, with zero experience on the ocean or with boats. But something in her tone made me throw caution to the wind. Why not? I had nothing holding me back. She told me a ticket would be waiting at the South Bend Regional Airport, Indiana, for Saturday, November 12. Without hesitation, I agreed—I'd be there.

The next day, Friday, November 11, I went to work with a gleam in my eye, the thought of warm, sunny Florida brightening the dullness of my routine. At the end of the day, I spoke to my boss, who immediately sensed something was up. He asked if I was quitting, and I confirmed it with a smile, thanking him for everything but letting him know I was off to a new adventure in Florida.

That evening, I headed to the University of Notre Dame with my brother and some friends for a Blues festival at the

Stepan Center. The music was great, but my mind was already on the adventure ahead. I was young, fearless, and ready to embrace whatever was coming, though I had no idea what I was really heading into.

Here's a snapshot of who we saw that night

Saturday, November 12 – Northern Indiana in November can get cold, grey, and dreary. I was more than ready to board that plane and leave it all behind. My girlfriend and a good buddy of mine, Hos, accompanied me to the airport that evening. It felt like a big moment—my first flight since 1959. I was born on an American Air Force base near Châteauroux, France, making me a military brat, but I hadn't been on a plane since my parents brought me to America at the age of two.

The flight from South Bend, IN, to Cleveland, Ohio, was a quick 45 minutes. I had a two-hour layover in Cleveland, where I took full advantage of the local laws that allowed 18-year-olds to drink "3.2 beer." I was in a party mood, feeling the thrill of the adventure ahead. Sitting in the airport bar, I could feel the excitement bubbling up as I sipped my beer, ready to start this new chapter.

Finally, it was time to board the flight to Fort Lauderdale. I remember the pilot's voice crackling over the speaker, announcing that the temperature in Florida was a balmy 70 degrees. It sounded like paradise compared to the cold I was leaving behind.

I dozed off during the flight, but when I woke up, it felt like someone had driven ice picks into my ears. The pain was excruciating—I had no idea that I should have worn earplugs to help with the pressure. It took a full 24 hours for the pressure to equalize and the pain to subside, but in that moment, I was just focused on enduring it.

When we landed, my mom and Roy-Boy were there to greet me at the Fort Lauderdale airport. We headed out for a few drinks and started talking about what was about to go down. There was a sense of excitement, but also an undercurrent of something more serious. As we finished up and made our way to the boat, the night had already fallen, so I couldn't see much of the vessel.

The boat, christened *The Mirage,* was docked at Pier 66. She was a 76-foot beauty that could sleep 12 to 14 people. Originally a shrimp boat, she had been converted into a yacht at some point. Even in the darkness, I could tell that this boat was something special. I fell in love with her instantly. But with a yacht comes a lot of maintenance—a lot of work. And as much as I admired *The Mirage*, I was still inexperienced and uncertain about what exactly my role would be.

The Mirage was a sight to behold—a 76-foot yacht, all white, with brown doors reminiscent of a tugboat. The wheelhouse was positioned up front, and everywhere you looked, there was beautiful tongue-and-groove woodwork. The white captain's chair in the wheelhouse gleamed, inviting anyone who sat in it to take command. For its time, the yacht was outfitted with top-notch technology: radar and sonar systems that scanned the front, back, and underneath, along with a CB radio and a high seas radio for communication.

She was more than just a boat; she was a marvel, and I could hardly believe my luck being there.

Right behind the wheelhouse, there was a cozy living room area complete with a couch and a TV. Beyond that was the galley—a compact kitchen outfitted with a modern stove and fridge, providing all the conveniences of home, just on a smaller scale. Even the doorways were small, which would later play a key role in my adventure.

The kitchen had tiled floors, a practical choice given the circumstances. We kept the doors open most of the time to let in the breeze, but the heat would inevitably invite the ocean to spray its way inside, making everything slick and slippery. On days when the weather took a turn for the worse, we'd close the doors tight, but honestly, I thrived in the heat—it made me feel alive.

Behind the kitchen, there was a cozy sitting area, complete with a table and a sliding glass door. It was a perfect spot to relax, catch a glimpse of the endless horizon, or just sit back and let the rhythm of the waves lull you into a state of calm.

The sitting area had indoor-outdoor carpet. Everything had to be secured tightly so that when the big swells hit things wouldn't end up toppling over or sliding off counters. Just beyond the dining area was a platform where you could fish or simply hang out and take in the vastness of the ocean. I spent countless hours there, soaking in the surroundings. The platform was about 8 by 16 feet, and at the back of the boat, there was a ladder leading down to another platform where the dinghies were kept, making it easy to access the water.

Below deck, the Mirage had four cabins—the master and three smaller sleeping quarters. They were small but comfortable, offering a cozy retreat from the relentless sea.

The heart of the Mirage was its three engines—two powerful diesel engines and a Chevy motor serving as a generator. The engine room was a world unto itself, with pumps constantly running and the temperature soaring. The heat was intense, and the diesel fumes were suffocating, making it a challenge to be down there for any length of time, especially when seasickness hit. And it hit me often. Seasickness, if you've never experienced it, is like being trapped in a never-ending hangover, with nausea, dizziness, and sometimes vomiting, all triggered by the relentless rocking and swaying of the vessel.

Sunday, November 13 - I woke up on the Mirage, still enveloped in the mysterious aura of our mission. The boat rocked gently, and the salty sea breeze mingled with the warmth of the sun. I could hardly believe I was here, soaking up this new reality. The sense of adventure was intoxicating.

The crew finally assembled to hear the plan. It was a small but eclectic team: Joe, the captain; Ron; Roy Boy; and me. Walter, the last member, would join us in a few days.

The plan was ambitious: we would sail from Ft. Lauderdale to Santa Marta, Colombia. Our cargo? A staggering 900 boxes of marijuana, each weighing 30 pounds. That's 27,000 pounds, or 13 and a half tons of weed—an almost inconceivable amount. The thought of handling that much marijuana was overwhelming.

The journey ahead promised to be grueling. Originally, there were five crew members, but one had dropped out, and that's when they called me. My musical talents were the main draw—I played drums, harmonica, banjo, saxophone, and acoustic guitar. They figured my skills would provide some much-needed entertainment on the long voyage. My strength and youth were also considered assets for the hard labor that lay ahead. Despite my eagerness, I was acutely aware that my inexperience might be a hindrance.

The boat had only a few regular weed smokers, but with the 70's in full swing, it seemed like everyone was dabbling in it. Looking back now, it's astonishing how much the world has changed - marijuana is now legal in many places, and its growth and use have evolved dramatically over the years.

Monday, November 14 - We start getting the boat stocked and ready. This beautiful, special boat. She had to be cleaned and prepped for her journey. I had no seamanship background whatsoever. I was lucky to be able to tie my own shoes, let alone one of those sailor knots. But I was going to give it my best shot. They were waving a lot of money in my face. I couldn't resist… NOPE!

Tuesday, November 15 – The preparations for the Mirage were in full swing, and everything seemed to be happening at lightning speed. There was an air of urgency as we hustled to get the yacht ready for the journey ahead. After a busy day of shopping for supplies—food, soda, cigarettes, and the like—I found myself at a mall in Ft. Lauderdale with my mom and Roy Boy. Our mission: to buy deck shoes, a must-have for anyone working on the boats down there.

As we walked through the entrance, a woman was coming out, holding the hands of two small, blond-haired boys. I couldn't help but pause for a moment, watching them. Without really thinking, I turned to my mom and said, "Someday, I'll have two boys of my own." It was a simple comment, but it stuck with me. That fleeting moment, those two little boys—they stayed in my mind, a quiet promise to myself that I would always remember.

Wednesday, November 16 – Our final day in Ft. Lauderdale had arrived, and the excitement was palpable. By now, I knew exactly how much money I'd be making on this trip, and the thought of it filled my mind with possibilities. That evening, we went out for dinner, but it wasn't just the meal that made the night memorable.

As we drove through the city, we passed by a Mercedes dealership, and there it was—the car of my dreams. A 450 SL coupe, sleek and shining under the showroom lights. I pointed it out immediately, saying, "That's the one I'm coming back to buy." It wasn't just wishful thinking; it was a promise to myself. We all believed we'd be coming back from this trip with a lot of cash in hand, and that car was going to be mine. The future felt so close I could almost touch it.

Thursday, November 17 – Our destination was Santa Marta, Columbia, but I was still in the dark about what lay ahead. Most of the crew had already been to Columbia before; everyone except Roy-Boy and me. As we were making the final preparations to set off, the last crew member finally arrived — Walter. He was a grizzled, experienced sailor who seemed to take an immediate dislike to me. In his eyes, I was too young, too green, with no real skills or stake in this game. All I had going for me was my enthusiasm, and that wasn't enough to impress Walter.

Before we could leave, one last task remained: pulling the dinghy, a top-of-the-line Zodiac, out of the water. Walter barked at me, "Jump down there and hook up the cable," expecting me to leap into action. But as I looked at the dark water below, swarming with jellyfish, I hesitated. I had no idea how to hook up the cable, and the thought of jumping in made my skin crawl. So I refused, saying, "Fuck that."

Walter didn't take my defiance well. He glared at me and spat out, "I'll do this for you one time, and I won't do it again!" The tension between us was immediate, and I knew we weren't off to a good start. Instead of showing me the ropes, he was being a prick right from the get-go.

I decided it was best to keep my mouth shut and my head down. As we finally got underway, heading for our first stop—Nassau in the Bahamas, 189 miles away—I couldn't help but glance back at the receding coastline and the twinkling lights of Ft. Lauderdale. Doubts crept in, but I knew I had to see this through. I had no idea what was in store for us, and at that moment, seasickness was the last thing on my mind.

The early part of the journey was calm. I stayed in the wheelhouse, eager to absorb as much as I could. Joe, the captain, was a seasoned pro and took me under his wing. He was patient, always willing to share his knowledge, and I liked him from the start.

We cruised at a steady nine knots, the boat cutting through the water with ease. Everything seemed calm and mellow. As the night settled in, I made my way downstairs. With only five of us on board, we had plenty of space to spread out and settle in for the night.

Friday, November 18 – I woke up to the steady hum of the Mirage slicing through the water, still on course to Nassau. I made my way back up to the wheelhouse. We all took turns at the wheel, each of us doing two-hour shifts to keep the Mirage moving. On for two hours, off for eight—not too bad, at least in the beginning. But as the waves grew larger, I started feeling a bit off. A slight queasiness crept in, and I wondered, *Is this seasickness?* I realized this journey might be tougher than I'd anticipated. The boat wasn't exactly breaking speed records, and Nassau still seemed far away.

Then, just as my stomach was turning knots, Nassau came into view. I'd heard tales of the island from friends, and now here it was, living up to every word. We navigated into the channel, with Paradise Island on our left and Nassau on our right. As we approached the port of entry, we had to pay the toll. They handed us a flag to fly while we were moored. Two men boarded the Mirage, and after a quick exchange of papers and a few dirty magazines, we were cleared to dock. It was 1977, and that's just how things were done.

Friday in Nassau, and we were finally docked, the Mirage proudly displaying all the necessary flags. The water was crystal clear, the sky an endless blue—such a stark contrast to the grey skies of Northern Indiana. I felt alive, soaking in the beauty of it all.

That evening, four of us—everyone except Walter— headed ashore for dinner. We took the Zodiac up the channel, tied it up, and ventured into town. I ordered shrimp fried rice, savoring the flavors and the freedom.

On our way back, we passed a massive ocean liner, towering above our little Zodiac. The sight was surreal, our small boat dwarfed by this giant vessel. Back on the Mirage, I decided to burn one down—no big deal getting high on this boat. Ron and Walter kept to themselves, rolling their own, which was fine by me.

Later that night, Joe, Ron, Roy Boy, and I decided to check out Paradise Island, just a half-mile across the channel. The island was home to a casino, and nobody bothered to check my ID. They didn't seem to care whether I was 21 or not. I didn't stay long—just pulled a few handles and drank a couple of beers. The thought of the big money waiting for me kept me grounded. They'd promised me $10,000 plus a bonus at the end of the run. Afterward, we'd be docking the Mirage in Freeport Bahamas, and I'd be in charge of taking care of her. It all felt too good to be true.

We returned to the Mirage to wind down for the night. I settled into my room downstairs, ready for whatever tomorrow might bring.

Saturday, November 19 – I woke up to the sound of a roaring engine, loud enough to shake the entire boat. Groggy, I peered out the porthole just in time to catch a seaplane bouncing along the water, getting ready to take off. It belonged to Chalks Airline, a service that operated between the Bahamas and Florida. Watching it lift off right out of the channel was the kind of moment that made you realize you were far from home—and it was the perfect way to start the day.

We decided to stick close to the Mirage that day, which meant plenty of time for some scuba diving. Earlier, I'd spotted a stingray glide gracefully under the boat, a gentle reminder that the waters here were alive with creatures I'd only ever seen on TV. Despite that, I suited up, determined to give diving a try.

Once in the water, though, I quickly realized I wasn't quite ready for this. The gear felt foreign, the water was deeper than it looked, and the vastness of the ocean hit me in a way I hadn't expected. I gave it a shot, but it was clear I needed more practice before I could really enjoy it. At least I tried.

The Mirage had this small area on top where we stored the dinghies, along with a few storage benches. It was a quiet spot, perfect for escaping the crew and finding a little peace. I had a stash of weed tucked away in a Pringles can that I'd take up there with me. There was something about watching the sunset from that perch, high above the water, that made everything feel just right. The world felt both infinite and small at the same time, and I soaked it all in, taking a few moments to myself before the next leg of our journey began.

Sunday, November 20 – We picked up a few more supplies and set our course for Staniel Cay Island. That's when things took a turn for me. As soon as we hit the open water, the waves began to toy with the Mirage, and my stomach was the first to surrender. The boat had no stabilizers, just rocking with the rhythm of the ocean, and once those swells started rolling, there was no escape.

The journey to Staniel Cay was only 83 miles, but to me, it felt like a marathon. Every minute dragged as I tried to hold it together. I took my turn at the wheel, but that was about all I could manage. The guys started calling me Lurch because I could barely stand. Crawling was the only way I could move without collapsing. My head was spinning, my stomach in knots. I was throwing up constantly, unable to get my bearings. The heat was relentless, and even the breeze that cut through the air was hot, offering no relief.

When my shift at the wheel ended—though it was more like babysitting the cruise control—Roy-Boy asked for help in the engine room. The idea of going down there, into that hot, diesel-scented hellhole, was almost impossible to fathom. But

I dragged myself down, determined to push through. It didn't go well. The combination of the heat, the fumes, and the endless rocking of the boat was too much. I did the best I could, but Walter wasn't impressed. He called me a "pansy-ass-pussy," but it didn't matter. I was beyond caring. Dramamine wasn't cutting it, and I was just trying to survive.

Later that night, we finally made it to Staniel Cay Island. It was dark, and I could barely make out the surroundings, too drained and sick to care much. We docked close to what I now know was the Yacht Club. Just as we were trying to settle in for the night, a crowd of 20 to 30 people suddenly appeared on the dock, eager to party on our boat. We were exhausted, sick, and in no mood for company. We had to shoo them away, just wanting a quiet place to dock and unwind after a grueling day. We were done, ready to call it a night and try to recuperate for whatever came next.

Monday, November 21 – I woke up the next morning and finally got a good look at the paradise we had docked in. Staniel Cay Island was simply breathtaking—pristine clear blue waters, untouched beaches that looked like something out of a dream. It was absolutely beautiful, and I couldn't believe I was actually there. The whole place had an almost magical quality, and for the first time in a while, I felt truly at ease. I was falling in love with Staniel Cay Island.

With the Mirage docked and the seasickness subsiding, I was starting to feel more like myself again. Joe, sensing the opportunity for a little adventure, suggested we visit the Grotto. If you've ever been to Staniel Cay, you'd know the Grotto. It's famous for being the location where they filmed scenes for the James Bond movie *Thunderball* back in the '60s. It was just the four of us again—Joe, Ron, Roy-Boy, and me. We piled into the Zodiac and motored over to the Grotto.

As we navigated inside, I was struck by how cool it was, like stepping into a movie set.

After the Grotto, we took the Zodiac out to explore another small, deserted island nearby. The Bahamas are dotted with these tiny islands, each one more beautiful than the last. We didn't know the name of this one, but it didn't matter. It was just us, surrounded by untouched nature, with no one else around. Walking along that island felt surreal—like I was part of something bigger, something special. It was hard to put into words, but everything was new to me, and I was buzzing with excitement. I was only 19, but I knew I was experiencing something most people never would.

Later, back on the Mirage, I decided to take a walk on my own. I rolled up a joint, stepped off the dock, and headed left up a massive hill with the ocean on my side. The climb was steep, but when I reached the top, the view took my breath away. I could see everything—no people, no distractions, just pure, unspoiled beauty. I lit up, let the smoke swirl around me, and just soaked it all in. This was one of the highlights of the trip for me. The sense of peace, the connection to the world around me—it was unforgettable.

I see pictures of Staniel Cay Island now, with pigs swimming in the water. I don't remember any pigs back then; they must've come later or been on a different part of the island. I'd love to go back someday, see how it's changed, and relive those moments. I know the Grotto would bring it all flooding back. I still can't believe how lucky I was. Music had opened doors for me all my life, but this… this was beyond anything I could have imagined.

Later that day, we set out to sea again. I asked Joe, "Where are we heading next?" He told me our next stop would be in

Haiti for fuel, and then we'd be docking in the capital, Port-au-Prince.

Tuesday, November 22 - The day stretched out before us with nothing but open water in every direction. The swells were relentless, rising and falling with a rhythm that caused a never-ending nausea. Each wave hit hard—lifting the boat high into the air before plunging it back down, again and again. It was during this stretch of the journey, halfway to Haiti, that I started questioning whether this trip was worth it. But it was far too late for second thoughts; there was no escape from the ride we were on. The swells were massive, the heat oppressive, and the constant drone of the engine seemed to echo in my head. Every eight hours, I'd take my turn at the wheel, guiding us through the monotonous cycle of chugging along at nine knots. The swells reached 10 to 12 feet at times, and then, out of nowhere, a rogue wave would crash into us, reminding me just how out of control things could get. This stretch of the journey would prove to be one of the toughest.

Wednesday, November 23 – Thursday, November 24 - The battle with the waves continued, and though I was still seasick, we were finally closing in on Haiti. We passed Cuba in the dead of night, never catching a glimpse, and made our way around the horn and into Haiti's horseshoe-shaped coastline. The waters remained rough, but I was slowly finding my sea legs, learning to move with the boat rather than against it. Walter, on the other hand, remained a thorn in my side, making every interaction a challenge. I knew he resented me for taking the place of his friend who backed out at the last minute. There's always one asshole in the group, and Walter filled that role perfectly. Ironically, though, he would later end up saving my life.

Friday, November 25 - I woke up to a change of pace—calm seas and bright sunshine as we cruised into Haiti's horseshoe bay. Our first order of business was to fuel up the Mirage. As we approached the fueling station, I noticed massive white fuel tanks lined up on the beach. We had to wait our turn, and it wasn't a quick process. Boats of all shapes and sizes were ahead of us, from yachts to fishing vessels to massive ocean liners. We were still a ways off from Port-au-Prince. While we waited, Walter and Joe brought out these large, black, rubber inner tubes—each about four or five feet in diameter and three feet high—to store extra fuel. We needed them topped off for the trip to Santa Marta and back to Miami, so we tied them down on top of the Mirage.

As we waited, I watched the locals working on the beach. Some waved at us, while a young woman jumped into the water to wash herself off. Before long, she climbed onto the dock and made her way onto our boat. The guys started laughing and egging her on, pointing toward me at the back of the boat. She approached me, saying, "Fucky-sucky five dollar," with a grin that sent a shiver down my spine. I quickly shook my head, saying, "No, no, I'm not doing that!" She wasn't exactly what I'd call attractive, and after days of seasickness, I wasn't in the best shape myself. We had to shoo her off the boat before things got any more awkward.

Here I am standing at the front of the Mirage as we were leaving the fueling station and heading to Port-au-Prince, Haiti.

As we docked at Port-au-Prince, the Point of Entry Guards boarded the Mirage. Joe handled the situation by slipping them some cash and a few dirty magazines in exchange for our paperwork and flag. By this point, I was utterly exhausted from the constant seasickness. I hadn't been able to eat or drink anything—not even water.

Port-au-Prince was a world apart from what I'd known. The Haitians were incredibly friendly and helpful; some even came aboard the Mirage to assist with much-needed repairs. The boat had taken a beating from the relentless waves and swells as we passed through the Atlantic Ocean into the Caribbean Sea. The water conditions were brutal, far beyond what I had anticipated, and every one of us had succumbed to seasickness at some point—except for Roy-Boy, who, with his Navy background, managed to handle it just fine. I, on the other hand, would end up losing close to 25 pounds over the course of the voyage.

As we approached the dock at Port-au-Prince, the first thing that struck me was a funky odor in the harbor—it lacked that fresh ocean-air smell I was used to. That initial impression set the tone for my experience in the capital.

Port-au-Prince, situated right in the middle of the horseshoe-shaped bay, is a sprawling city teeming with boats of all kinds—fishing boats, ocean liners, you name it. We managed to blend in and tied up at the dock. For Walter, Joe, and Ron, this was familiar territory—they had made this run before. But for Roy-Boy and me, it was an entirely new experience. Walter had connections in Haiti, people ready to assist us with getting around and working on the boat. One older Haitian man, in particular, was incredibly kind, and I got to know him pretty well. The poverty in Haiti was evident everywhere we went, but despite having so little, the people were warm and eager to help us with repairs.

The Mirage had really taken a pounding from the big waves. I can't stress enough how challenging it was to navigate those waters—the storms and swells made it a serious, demanding journey. Everyone was feeling the strain, but we were getting closer to our destination. Once we had the boat in order, Walter and Joe went out to gather supplies. I asked them to bring me some 7-Up or something similar, and they returned with a knock-off brand called "UP," which I gulped down gratefully. They also brought back supplies for our Thanksgiving dinner that night.

I had been so sick that the thought of food was unappealing, but the guys managed to throw together a meal. We all gathered around the dining table. I have a picture from that night—Walter holding the knife, Ron, Joe, and me at the table. Everyone was tanned from working out in the sun constantly—everyone except for me. I looked as pale as the white shirt I was wearing. As they say, a picture is worth a thousand words, and that one clearly showed the hell I had been through. But I'm glad I have that picture. If it weren't for Roy-Boy, who took those photos all those years ago, I'd have nothing to look back on.

Saturday, November 26 - We began the day by working on the Mirage—cleaning, organizing, repairing—anything that needed attention. A couple of the Haitians who had helped us before returned to lend a hand.

Later on, Joe, Ron, Roy-Boy, and I decided to explore Port-au-Prince. Walter had arranged for a car and driver, so we had a way to get around. Being a white guy from the States, I stood out like a cue ball, but the Haitians were friendly and welcoming toward tourists. They were eager to sell us anything they had, just as they did with the ocean liners that docked in the harbor. The locals would line the docks with their merchandise, ready to sell their wares to the tourists as they stepped on shore.

It was a beautiful day—clear blue skies—and for once, I wasn't seasick. It felt like a good day. As we drove around, we stopped at a small shop—more of a shack or hut—where an artist crafted items from mahogany wood. Roy-Boy picked up four carvings that I've kept over the years.

Next, we drove up into the hills outside of Port-au-Prince to visit a rum factory. Being only 19, (and finally feeling good for a change) I was ready to have some fun. The rum factory was an impressive structure, made of rock and stone, like an old fort or castle. We took a tour of the rum-making process, and afterward, we went outside to sample the different flavors. The tasting area was on a ledge or balcony at the back of the factory, overlooking the hills. Below us, children were singing and dancing for the tourists, hoping for a few coins. It was heartbreaking to see the poverty they lived in, but they were still full of energy and joy. We tossed down some quarters and watched as they scrambled to collect the change.

After leaving the rum factory, we stopped at a small restaurant built into the side of a cliff. From our table, we had a breathtaking view of the entire harbor. Although I was feeling better, I still felt as if I were on the boat—the sensation of waves and rocking hadn't left me. I wasn't ready to eat much, but I thoroughly enjoyed the view and the atmosphere. After our meal, we headed back to the Mirage.

As we drove through Port-au-Prince, it started to rain. The downpour washed sewage from the shacks and huts in the hills down into the streets and eventually into the harbor. The smell was overwhelming—a pungent reminder of the poverty I had witnessed. It's the kind of experience that stays with you, something that words can't fully capture.

When we returned to the Mirage, the boat looked much better after all the work we had put into it. The fuel tanks were full and securely strapped down, and the galley was stocked and ready. We settled in for the night, but I couldn't stand to go outside because of the unbearable smell.

Sunday, November 27 - The following morning, the elderly Haitian man who had helped us with the repairs brought me a gift. It was a beautifully crafted mahogany cigarette holder, a piece of craftsmanship so fine that I still have it to this day. Whenever I tap it for good luck, I think of that kind old man and his generosity.

I didn't think I had anything to give him in return, but I managed to find some T-shirts I had packed. When I handed them to him, he seemed genuinely appreciative. It was clear that they had very little there, and even something as simple as a T-shirt was valuable.

With repairs done and goodbyes exchanged, we finally set off toward our destination—Santa Marta, Colombia. I took my turn in the wheelhouse around 1:00 or 2:00 in the afternoon. The waters were still calm as we made our way to the northwest tip of Haiti before turning south. Everything was on cruise control, so all I had to do was keep an eye on the course. I settled into the big Captain's Chair and began playing my harmonica.

For those who play the harmonica, it was a Hohner diatonic Golden Melody in the key of F. I played a few tunes, and for the first time in a while, I felt a sense of peace. It seemed like everything was finally falling into place. But as it turned out, that would be the last time I played my harmonica on this journey.

Later that night, while I was sleeping in the lounge area, we rounded the corner near Dame Marie, Haiti, and hit open water. That's when all hell broke loose. The fuel tanks we had secured on top came loose and fell off. We lost all three. The waves became violent so quickly it was as if someone had flipped a switch. Suddenly, it was back to the harsh reality of our voyage. That night felt endless.

Monday, November 28 – Wednesday, November 30 - The journey to Santa Marta was a relentless battle. The battering never let up—nothing but deep, open waters as far as the eye could see. The Caribbean Sea was unyielding, throwing wave after wave at us. I had to crawl everywhere on the boat because the waves were so high. Despite the conditions, we continued taking turns in the wheelhouse, doing our best to maintain our course.

I was right back where I started with the seasickness. I couldn't even keep water down. The constant nausea and exhaustion made me second-guess this entire trip. I began to wonder if this adventure was the great idea I had imagined it to be. All I could do was watch the boat rise and fall, up and down, over and over again. The monotony was maddening, and the journey seemed endless.

Thursday, December 1 – The details of that day are a bit hazy, but what I do remember is that we finally made it to Santa Marta that night. The shore was lined with lights, a sight that brought a sense of relief after the long journey. Joe was on the CB, communicating with someone named Carlos. They had pre-arranged code words, so Carlos knew who we were. Out of nowhere, a speedboat pulled up beside us, and a guy climbed onto the back platform and up the ladder. It was

Carlos. I liked him immediately—he was a really nice guy and clearly in control of everything at Santa Marta.

Carlos took over the CB, switched channels, and started speaking rapid Spanish to some guys on the other end. Then he directed Joe on where to go for the pickup. After 15 days and approximately 1,622 miles, we had finally reached our destination. We were here to pick up some of the best dark brown Colombian bud I had ever seen. It was rare to come across that in Northern Indiana, where we called it Colombian Gold, but this was something else—coffee brown, premium, and it smelled incredible.

Carlos continued giving instructions in Spanish and then told Joe in English how to navigate. Suddenly, small speedboats began arriving, pulling up to the doors on either side of the Mirage, as well as at the back. For about three hours, boat after boat brought 20 or more boxes at a time. We filled every inch of the Mirage with those boxes until you could barely move inside her. Even the lounge, where I had been sleeping and finding some semblance of comfort, was packed full. It had become my refuge, the only place where I felt halfway decent.

In the end, we had loaded 900 boxes of marijuana—over 13 and a half tons. It was unbelievable how much we had on that boat, but at the time, I didn't give it a second thought.

During the loading process, a generator on shore broke down. Roy-Boy, ever the helpful one, jumped onto one of the speedboats and went ashore to help fix it. He was the only one of us who actually set foot on land in Santa Marta. The rest of us stayed on the Mirage, focused on getting everything loaded while Joe and Walter settled up with Carlos.

Looking back, I realize how risky that operation was, but at the time, it seemed like just another part of the adventure. There were plenty of boats out there doing the same thing, though I'm sure you couldn't get away with it now. My experience with the people in Santa Marta was a good one—they treated the whole thing as a business transaction and treated us well.

Once Roy-Boy was back onboard and everything was loaded, we set our course for Miami. But this was where things started to turn on us. It was the beginning of the end.

Friday, December 2 – Joe, our Captain, was supposed to head back around the east side of Cuba, retracing the route we had originally taken. But for reasons unknown to me, he made the decision to go north-northwest, along the west side of Cuba. Even now, I can't fathom why he chose to change our course. That Friday morning would turn out to be the most perilous part of the journey for me. My shift at the wheel began at 6 AM, with Walter waking me up. I was feeling off, battling the relentless waves, just eager to get home and collect my money. The Mirage was heaving back and forth, up and down in the sweltering heat. I stopped in the galley to take some Dramamine. Both doors on either side of the galley were wide open, allowing water to spray in and drench the floor. As I reached into the fridge for something to wash down the pills, a massive rogue wave hit us out of nowhere! It slammed into the Mirage, throwing me hard to the right, then backward, sending me flying through the open door. At the last possible second, I spread my arms wide and managed to catch myself in the doorway. Thank God the doors were so narrow—if they hadn't been, I would have been flung overboard, and no one would have realized I was gone for hours. The boat pitched in the opposite direction, tossing me to the floor. Trembling from what had just happened, I somehow made it up to the wheelhouse. I told Walter how I'd nearly been thrown off the boat, and he just laughed. He thought it was hilarious. Then he said, "Get your ass on that wheel and take your turn." And that was that. I had survived another day, but that was the closest I ever came to falling off that damn boat and drowning.

Saturday, December 3 – We kept pushing northward through the Caribbean Sea. The water was extremely rough, with waves towering over us. The Mirage was heavily loaded and had to plow through some massive swells. But we were making headway. If I wasn't on the wheel, I was lying down, trying to recover. It was all I could manage.

Sunday, December 4 – My shift on the wheel started first thing in the morning. Everything seemed to be running smoothly. After my shift, I headed back to the lounge to rest on the floor. Around noon, though, something felt off. I had been dozing, but you can always tell when you're moving by the rhythm of hitting the waves, and suddenly, that rhythm stopped. I got up and went to the back of the boat, where I saw Joe and Walter in a panic. The Mirage was just sitting there, rocking in the waves, but not making any forward progress. Joe and Walter were suiting up in their scuba gear to check what was going on. It was a dangerous task with the boat rocking so violently, but they managed to get underwater to inspect the damage. When they climbed back onto the platform, they looked at us and said, "Our prop shaft has snapped in two." Many yachts have two props, but the Mirage only had one. Was it the weight of the weed? The relentless pounding of the waves? Or Joe's decision to head northwest instead of east? It didn't matter now. We were drifting, helpless.

Joe quickly got on the high-seas radio to contact our people back home. He had to be extremely cautious with what he said—anyone could be listening. He couldn't disclose our location. All he could say was that we had mechanical issues and were adrift.

Monday, December 5 – The first few days of drifting were incredibly rough. We started rationing our water and food because we had no idea how long we'd be out there. I was still battling seasickness, and now we weren't even making any progress. I can't recall if it was Monday or Tuesday, but Joe and Walter called me up to the wheelhouse. When I got there, they told me to look toward the northeast. I could barely make it out, but they were pointing out Jamaica to me. From that point, we started drifting toward Honduras and Nicaragua. The gravity of our situation hadn't quite sunk in for me yet.

Tuesday, December 6, – It was my 20th birthday. I remember telling Roy Boy that I'd never forget this birthday— drifting on that damn boat. I didn't even smoke or eat anything that day. I wandered up to the bow of the boat. The flying fish kept landing on the front, and I had to kick them back over the side as I made my way up. I had dry heaves, as usual. But then I threw up over the side, and the wind caught it and blew it right back into my face. That was it. I was done—with the trip, the boat, the money. All I wanted was to make it back home. Some birthday, huh?

Wednesday, December 7 – Things started to calm down a bit for me. The waves didn't seem quite as bad, and I wasn't feeling as sick. I almost felt a little hungry. I put some peanut butter on a spoon and dipped it in a big jar of honey. That filled me up and gave me a sugar boost all in one go. The only drinks left were Coke or water—no bottled water back in those days. But I could tell I was starting to feel a little better. I was finally getting my sea legs.

We were still drifting, so I decided to try my hand at fishing during the day. I had to find something to do. The waves had calmed down, and things were becoming more manageable. Joe showed me how to set up the reels and get started.

As soon as I cast my line, something huge grabbed it and took off. It snapped my steel line like a rubber band. Joe helped me set up the pole again, and I got another bite. This time, we could see it—a hammerhead shark. He must've been 7 or 8 feet long from what I could tell. We took turns fighting this beast for over an hour. I kept saying, "All I want is the teeth." I needed something to show for all I'd been through. But eventually, the shark moved toward the bow, and soon enough, *SNAP*—the line broke, and he was gone.

We did catch other fish, though. Plenty of small Tiger sharks, Shark-suckers (which we used for bait), and Mahi-Mahi (dolphinfish). Those were REALLY tasty. They're blue in the water but turn yellow when you pull them out—that blew me away.

That evening, we had a meeting. We realized we couldn't stay on this boat forever. Joe used the high-seas radio to call his contact in the States again, talking to whoever was fronting this operation, trying to pull a plan together.

Later that night, after finally getting my appetite back, I watched the sunset while burning a fatty, listening to Walter's cassette player. That's all there was to do. No cell phones to play with back then.

Thursday, December 8 – By now, I had my sea legs under me pretty well. I was cooking more and eating the fish we caught. I'd never been deep-sea fishing in my life, but I was giving it my all now, trying to make the best of a tough situation. Walter and I were sitting at the back of the boat early in the day when I spotted a strange-looking fish. It was puffed up, with spikes sticking out, floating on top of the water—just amazing. Walter thought it was a blowfish or pufferfish.

It rained off and on during the day. Joe showed me how to use the rainwater to shower so we could conserve our other water for drinking. The rain would run off the side of the roof, and we'd stand under the corner of the upper deck at the stern, letting the rainwater run over us. Joe taught me a lot on this trip, and I was grateful he was there.

That evening, I was back to listening to Walter's cassette player—J. Geils Band, Jackson Browne, and Rod Stewart were all I had, and Ron had a Jeanne Pruett cassette. I heard "Satin Sheets" a few times, needless to say, but it was all good. I rolled one up, sat on the port side of the boat, and listened to Rod Stewart's *Atlantic Crossing*. The waves weren't so bad that night. It was pretty calm. I just enjoyed the music, watched the sunset, and marveled at the stars. Oh my God, the stars were everywhere—what a sight. I loved it.

Later that night, Joe called me up to the wheelhouse. As I looked at the radar, it showed something really big headed our way. We didn't have the Mirage's running lights on—I'm not sure if we were conserving energy or just afraid of being spotted. But this huge thing turned out to be a cargo ship. It seemed like it was right next to us as it passed by. That's when I started to realize just how dangerous this drifting really was!

Friday, December 9 – I could feel the tension building—there was no denying it. We had to find a way off this boat. Nobody was coming to save us, and if we didn't get out of there, we'd end up in jail. That morning, Joe and Walter made the bold decision to jump into the Zodiac and head to shore. We could see land, but it was pretty far off, and at that point, I wasn't even sure where we were. They left early in the morning and didn't get back until late in the afternoon. It took a lot of guts to jump into that little dinghy in those rough waters, but they came back with a plan. They told us that tomorrow we'd sink the Mirage and head to Honduras on the Zodiacs. While on the beach, they'd seen a path leading inland, and that's where we would go.

We started looking for anything we could salvage and take with us on the Zodiacs, but it wasn't much. I even had to leave my harmonicas behind. That afternoon, I was standing on top of the boat with Joe and Walter, getting the two dinghies ready when someone suggested we should take a swim before heading to shore. Joe, Roy-Boy, Ron, and Walter all jumped over the side. I thought, "Sure, why not?" But at the last minute, I hesitated, thinking about what might be in that water—I had just seen an 8-foot hammerhead swimming around us the other day. I decided I wasn't jumping in there. But Walter had other plans and said, "Oh yes, you are!" He started coming after me, so I ran and jumped into the

Caribbean Sea, swimming as fast as I could to the platform at the back of the boat to get my ass out of that water. They all thought that was pretty funny.

That night, we decided to cook up everything we had for one last meal. We even emptied out the big freezer. There was so much food that I started throwing it to the birds. There were always plenty of birds following us—pelicans, seagulls, Man-of-War birds, and others I couldn't identify. They ate well that night. I enjoyed feeding the birds and taking in all the sea life around us. It was so peaceful. We all gathered at the back of the Mirage and watched the sunset for the last time. It was beautiful—the water, the sunset, the night sky, and the stars. The whole experience was something I didn't fully appreciate at the time. I just didn't realize what a surreal moment that really was.

Saturday, December 10 – What a day… It was finally time to get off that damn boat. The morning was beautiful—blue skies and manageable waves. Joe and Walter had gone ashore the day before to check everything out, and they decided it was time to sink the Mirage and head for land. After six days of floating with all that weed, we all knew it was time to go.

Roy-Boy and I were in one dinghy, while Joe, Walter, and Ron were in the other. We shut off all the pumps, opened all the windows and doors, and did everything we could to sink the Mirage. At least, I thought that was the plan. We were still quite a distance from the shore, and the waves were pretty big. This went on for a few hours but felt like much longer. We kept circling the Mirage, waiting. Eventually, it was about halfway down in the water, and by that time, the boxes were starting to float out of the windows. It became clear that those boxes weren't going to sink—they were sealed in plastic wrap.

Then, a fishing boat came along. The crew saw we were in trouble and wanted to help. We ended up getting on the fishing boat, which was a lot bigger than the Mirage. They must have known what was going on. We asked them to ram the Mirage to sink it. They hit it three or four times, which was one hell of a thing to witness—all those boxes of weed floating while they rammed the Mirage,. Then, we asked them to take us to shore, to Honduras. As I turned around for one last look, the Mirage was still half in and half out of the water. It was so sad to see her floating like that. She was a beauty. To this day, I believe those fishermen went back and tried to save her and salvage what they could, but I'll never know if they did.

When you're in a boat and looking at land, you think you're much closer than you actually are. In reality, it took us a few hours to get to shore. Finally, we were getting off the fishing boat and heading for land. We took very little with us. We'd had guns, but we gave them to the fishermen as thanks for giving us a lift to shore. And we told them to keep the dinghies—they did pretty well for themselves that day.

So, we made it to shore in Honduras. It was maybe 1 or 2 in the afternoon. I was so glad to be back on land after 24 days and over 2,740 miles on the ocean.

This map gives you an idea of what this journey covered.

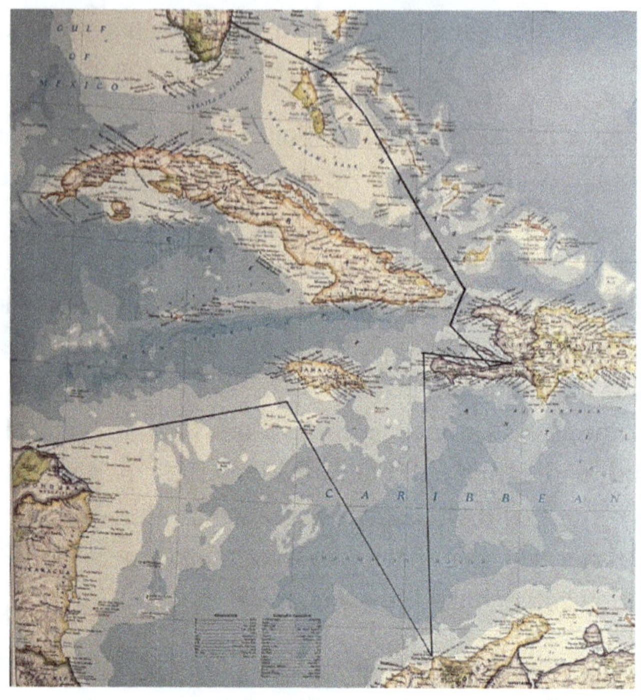

The fishermen told us there was an airport nearby, maybe two or three miles inland. But as soon as we got off the beach, we were in a thick, green jungle. There was a path, and we were told it would take us to a village with an airport. It took about 45 minutes of walking to get there. Sometimes, we had to go through water, holding our packs above our heads, just like in a jungle movie. I didn't even want to think about the snakes, spiders, or any other critters that might be in that jungle—I just wanted to keep moving.

We finally came to a small village. We saw a runway in the clearing, but there were no planes around, and it was a very small dirt airstrip. We ate at the only café—very primitive— and told the local villagers that our boat hit something and sank. We had to tell them something—five Americans don't just show up in a village like this on a stroll. The people were so friendly and helpful, but we couldn't tell them exactly what had gone down. They told us planes only landed in this village once in a while. They said we'd have a better chance if we went to a bigger village. They also mentioned a "boat" in the channel that would take us to the river and on to a bigger village where we could make arrangements to get to an airport and back to the States. But it was miles away. In my mind, I thought I'd be going home real soon—maybe the next day. We just hung out by the café with the locals that day. We even smoked some weed with them that evening. They treated us really well.

Later that night, the "boat" showed up. It was actually a 30-foot canoe carved out of a huge tree, with a canopy over the top and a motor on the back. It could hold maybe 8 to 10 people. By this time, it was pitch dark, making it hard to see, but I was ready to go—whatever it took. As we were getting settled and moving down the channel, the boat started to tip hard to the left. I thought we were all going in the river and braced myself, getting ready to jump in. The captain yelled for everyone to sit down. That was a very tense moment, but things stabilized, and we were off again, heading into the darkness with the feeling of, "Here we go."

It took a couple of hours to get to the "bigger village," and the airport wasn't exactly what we'd call an airport. It was Saturday night, but the planes only came once a week on Saturday morning, so we missed it. This day had been crazy from beginning to end, and now we were going to have to wait a week for the next Saturday.

We were told the village had a small hotel where we could stay. Some hotel… No consistent electricity, just a generator that the village fired up at night for a few hours. The bathroom was outside, as were the showers, but at least it was a room to sleep in. Roy-Boy and I stayed in a room together. As we walked by Walter's room, we heard buzzing—mosquitos! His room was full of them. The hotel manager came up and said, "I'll take care of it." He went in, sprayed something, and a few minutes later, the mosquitos were gone. But there were no lights, no AC, no fan. We were roughing it for the week, but at least we were still alive.

We decided to go to the bar and get a drink. It was just a shack, but I was definitely ready for a drink. It was the only bar in the village. I thought maybe some of the locals would hassle us—they looked us over but didn't give us any trouble. We didn't have much money, but Roy-Boy had grabbed the CB radio off the Mirage at the last minute even though Joe and Ron had told him not to take it. It would save our asses later when he was able to sell it.

Sunday, December 11 – We walked around the village in the morning to get a feel for where we were. The village had dirt roads, mostly lined with shacks with thatch roofs, and a few cement block buildings like our hotel. We found a place to eat—the only place to eat. We would eat there twice a day, once in the morning and once in the afternoon, for the entire time we were there. That was it. Lots of beans, rice, and chicken. Just as primitive as you can imagine. They had wild, colorful birds as pets, and those birds were everywhere. They were loud, but we got used to it.

Monday, December 12 – The judge/magistrate of the village asked to talk to us. He wanted to speak to each of us separately. I'm sure he was skeptical of our story. His office was in the back of a shack at the airstrip. I was very nervous going into that back room to talk with him. Roy-Boy and Walter had told me to say as little as possible. I was the last one called in to talk to him, and I didn't say much. He asked for my ID, and I happened to have a police ID from my hometown. He asked if I was part of the police force there, and I lied and said yes. But even with that, we were not allowed to leave the village—not that there was any way to leave. There was no way you could walk out through this jungle. The judge decided that one of us would be allowed to fly out on the following Saturday—just one. Walter was picked to go and try to make arrangements to get the rest of us out.

Tuesday, December 13 – Friday, December 16 – Without much money, there wasn't much we could do. We just stayed near our hotel rooms. I wasn't in the best mood, realizing I wasn't going to make any money on this trip. I just kept my head down, waiting to get the hell out of there. You don't know how much you miss the States until you're not able to get back home.

Saturday, December 17 – First thing in the morning, I heard the plane coming. We all headed down to the dirt airstrip to see Walter off. I remember shaking Walter's hand as he was getting on the plane, and he looked at me with that shit-eating grin. I never saw him again after that. You know… Walter was right all along. I had no business being on that boat.

Sunday, December 18 – Tuesday, December 20 – So, what do we do while we're waiting to see if Walter can get us home? By this time, we were running low on money. We had no idea we'd be there so long. As we walked around the village, we met three other Americans. One was with the Peace Corps. The other two said they had a boat they were working on in the harbor, but I have no idea what they were actually doing down there. Roy-Boy was able to sell them the CB radio he had taken off the Mirage. If he hadn't brought that, we never would have had enough money to eat that week.

Wednesday, December 21 – Here is where the story gets even wilder. One of the Americans we met in that village was actually from our hometown. Now, what are the chances of that? Being in the middle of the jungle and running into someone who is from your hometown. I remember Roy-Boy coming back to our hotel room and telling me this guy was from home. I laughed and didn't believe him. But he ended up giving Roy-Boy a letter to take back to his mother when—if— we ever made it out

Thursday, December 22 – Friday, December 23 – At that point, I was getting pretty nervous. I wasn't sure how we were going to get home. Was Walter going to be able to arrange something for us? Money was running low, and walking out was definitely not an option. My appetite was coming back, though. Off the boat and feeling better, but just waiting...

I remember walking through the village with Ron and deciding to climb up a coconut tree to grab a coconut. I came back down, broke it open, and ate some fresh coconut. You don't get to do that every day.

Friday night was supposed to be our last night in the village, and I was so ready to get home. Things were really tight—we had spent all our money by then.

When Walter left, he said the airplane he would send for us would circle the village twice before landing. That's how we would know it was ours because there would be other planes coming that day too.

Saturday, December 24 – Christmas Eve – Time was running out. We packed everything we had, and sure enough,

Saturday morning, we heard a plane circle the village twice. We were all ready to go! It was a good hike from the hotel to the airstrip, and I remember how happy I was, waving to some of the villagers and thanking them for helping us.

We arrived at the judge's office at the airstrip after the plane had landed, but the airport manager told us it wasn't our plane. Then, a man stepped off the plane and walked into the waiting area where we were. He held up his hand, signaling us to wait. He was dressed in a suit and tie, carrying a briefcase, and looked like he meant business. He went into the back room with the judge and shut the door. He wasn't in there long. When he came out, he simply said, "Let's go." He didn't have to say it twice. I'm sure he paid the judge off to get us out of there. The judge knew something shady had happened, and he got paid to keep quiet. To this day, I have no idea how much it took to get us out, but that judge probably made more money from this trip than any of us did.

The plane was a small, six-passenger, single-engine aircraft. I can't describe the relief I felt as we took off out of that village. As we hit the runway, the man who bailed us out offered us cigarettes, candy, and something to drink. I was starving, having been living off village food and coconuts, and we were out of cash.

It took a few hours to reach the capital of Honduras, Tegucigalpa. I just remember looking down and seeing nothing but a blanket of thick green jungle until we reached the Tegucigalpa airport. There was really no way we could have walked out of that village.

The airport we landed at in the capital was in the middle of a big valley, surrounded by huge mountains. It was something to see.

After landing, we went to the lounge and finally had tickets for home! We would be flying into Miami later that night. The gentleman with the briefcase, who had gotten us out of the village, turned out to be a lawyer. Walter had met with him the previous Saturday after leaving the village and had told him about our situation. Despite all the trouble I'd had with Walter, he had actually saved my ass. Throughout the entire trip, I never asked where the money was coming from to fund this adventure. Someone back in the States was behind it all, but I never knew who. I imagine they put up the money that was paid to get us out. Like I said, I have no idea who it was, and some things are just best left alone. But we were told someone wired the money to the lawyer, and he came, paid the judge off, and got us out of there.

Now, we were sitting in the Tegucigalpa airport lounge, just waiting to go to Miami. After everything I'd been through—seasickness, ten to twelve-foot swells, rogue waves, almost flying off the boat in the early morning hours, the Mirage breaking down, drifting for over six days, two weeks in a jungle village—thirty-eight days later, we were finally going home.

We had stops in three other countries that evening: El Salvador, Guatemala, and Belize. Two of the airports had big anti-aircraft guns on the runway. Like I said, I'm trying to remember everything I had seen on this trip.

We finally got to Miami late that night, Christmas Eve 1977. My mom and Ron's wife picked us up at the airport. Mom couldn't believe how much weight I had lost, but it was finally over. We dropped Joe off at a bar in Hollywood, Florida. That was the last time I ever saw him.

We went back to Ron's house in Ft. Lauderdale to regroup. I didn't see much of Ron after that. We started driving back to Northern Indiana that night. I think it finally hit Roy-Boy that we weren't making any money from this adventure, and he was ready to get home. We all were. When we reached home, he fulfilled his promise and delivered the letter to the mother of the guy we had met back in the village.

As I look back on this trip after all these years, I think about what might have happened if we had made it back to Miami with our cargo. We might have even gotten busted there. Who knows?

At the beginning of this adventure, when my mom and I were shopping at the Ft. Lauderdale Mall, I told her that someday I would be married and have two boys of my own. And that's exactly what I did.

Jacob, Dale, and Michael Ballard

We lost Roy-Boy in 1992. My mom passed away just 22 months later in 1994

Mom and Roy-Boy at Flagler Bar in the Bahamas, 1977 (Livin' The Life)

I'd go on to work a lot of different jobs. I eventually put my own blues band together called Catman and the All-Niters and put out two CD's. And I'm still playing off and on.

Here is a picture of one of the 2,500 plus shows of my music career.

My mom in front of the Mirage, 1977

After it's all said and done, everybody has their run in life. But this was… MY Caribbean Run.

www.ingramcontent.com/pod-product-compliance
Lightning Source LLC
Chambersburg PA
CBHW061102050726

47592CB00004B/1790